# Humility

*The* Quiet Virtue

EVERETT L. WORTHINGTON JR.

Templeton Foundation Press

Philadelphia & London

Templeton Foundation Press
300 Conshohocken State Road, Suite 670
West Conshohocken, PA 19428
www.templetonpress.org

Templeton Foundation Press helps intellectual leaders and others learn
about science research on aspects of realities, invisible and intangible.
Spiritual realities include unlimited love, accelerating creativity, worship,
and the benefits of purpose in persons and in the cosmos.

Library of Congress Cataloging-in-Publication Data
Worthington, Everett L., 1946-
Humility : the quiet virtue / Everett L. Worthington, Jr.
p.   cm.
Includes bibliographical references.
ISBN-13: 978-1-59947-128-0 (pbk. : alk. paper)
ISBN-10: 1-59947-128-0 (pbk. : alk. paper)   1.  Humility.  I. Title.

BJ1533.H93W67 2007
179'.9—dc22                    2007024127
WORTHINGTON
Designed and typeset by Helene Krasney
Printed in the United States of America

07 08 09 10 11 12  10 9 8 7 6 5 4 3 2 1

*To Rena Canipe, hero of humility, and to all of her family, who hold her identity together in love.*

# Contents

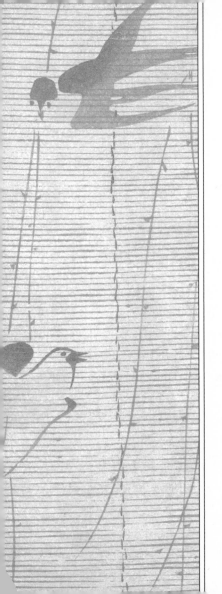

We rise in glory
as we sink in pride.

—ANDREW YOUNG

# Introduction

WRITING A BOOK ON HUMILITY is fraught with difficulties. I certainly do not want to write a book with the invisible sub-title "My Humility and How I Achieved It Perfectly." I am not even inviting you to dwell on your own humble traits. I cannot tell you a definitive description of humility revealed by science. A scientific understanding of humility simply does not exist at this point, and it is hampered by the paradox of measuring humility. Asking a respondent to rate how humble he or she is is an exercise in futility.

To help you understand humility, I can only invite you to consider people you know. Who are your heroes of humility? Write down your nominations for your Hall of Humility. Then, consider each one. What characteristics made you choose each person as a hero? Perhaps in reflecting on your heroes of humility, you will understand what makes up humility.

This is the tack I use in this book. I will describe people like Rena Canipe—just folks—who embody world-class humility, and I'll follow Rena's story as to whether she can win the battle against the humiliation of dementia. I will examine people of great achievement who exude humility, look to historical figures whose humility has stood the test of time, and describe a few fictional stories whose protagonists inspire us to humility. I will peek at what science has found in studying humility. I have scoured sources of wise quotes about humility and selected some that I hope will inspire you.

If together we examine these exemplars of humility, perhaps we might forge a common understanding of, at a minimum, how humility shows up. Humility doesn't shout its characteristics. It is the quiet virtue. We must approach it in reverence. Because it is quiet, we must listen, look, and feel to discern its character.

Why are you reading this book about humility? Probably not to hone your humility skills so you can win an award for humility. You are probably not looking for the praise and adoration of thousands. In fact, I would bet that you already are humbly serving others, and you are seeking inspiration that will fortify your life choices.

Typically, a book's introduction or first chapter tries to motivate the reader to learn more. In a way, this book cannot be traditional because I believe that, if you are reading this little text, you already have the motivation and the experience that you will uncover in these pages. But I believe there is strength in like-motivated communities. I hope to strengthen you through quotes about humility from wise people. I hope you will apply what you read to your own life, find your own heroes of humility, and be inspired by those heroes to greater acts of love and virtue than you may ever have dreamed about doing already.

# Humility

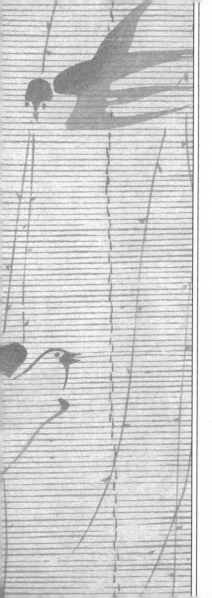

Humility does not mean thinking less of yourself than of other people, nor does it mean having a low opinion of your own gifts. It means freedom from thinking about yourself at all.

—WILLIAM TEMPLE

# Paradoxes and Potentials
# of Humility

MOST OF THE HEROES of humility in my life I have known from afar. This one I know intimately. Hers is a story of humility and her battle against humiliation. At ninety years old, she has progressive dementia, and she is descending into the same humiliation faced by many who see their personalities slipping away.

*At 5:00 a.m. on a July morning in 1978, Rena Canipe crawled out of her bed in Lake Park, Florida, in the West Palm Beach area. She awakened her husband Clyde. Donning their track suits, they climbed into their old Volkswagen bus and headed to the mall near their home. Behind a grocery store, one of the managers was awaiting their morning visit. The day-old food was ready to be dumped, but Rena had*

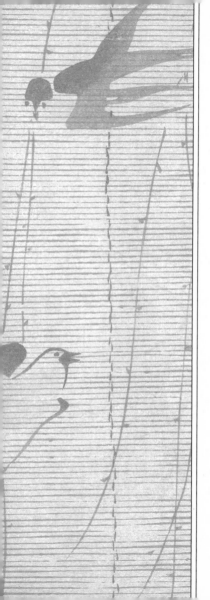

By foreign hands thy
humble grave adorned;
By strangers honored, and
by strangers mourned.

—ALEXANDER POPE

convinced the manager that the food could be put to much better use to feed shut-ins who had difficulty getting to the store. They loaded the VW bus all the way to the top of the passenger and cargo areas.

Rena and Clyde began their first of five trips throughout southern Florida. By 2:00 p.m., the last of the food had been delivered, and Rena and Clyde had their first meal of the day. This routine went on for years before new management nixed it.

Clyde was a retired school principal. Rena had devoted her life to motherhood and volunteer service. In 1998, she was recognized by the Palm Glades Girl Scout Council with the Rena Canipe Keep-the-Faith Award, and in 2000, was featured in the Girl Scout calendar. She has served many people in many ways over the course of her life. She did this work neither for money nor for the few awards and recognition that have come her way as the result of her service.

If you have watched Rena in action for over thirty-five years, as I have, as her son-in-law, you realize that she has helped thousands of people through food delivery, as a scout leader, as consultant to the Girl Scouts, at church, and through acquaintances. Yet, in those thirty-five years, she never has told me about all of her efforts. She served in silence. "I've never done anything important in my life," said Rena.

5

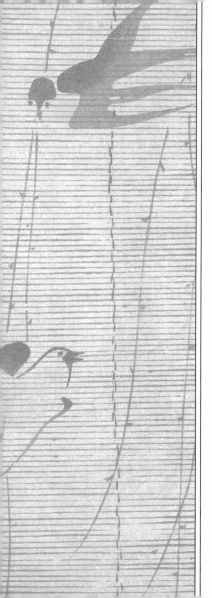

Do nothing out of selfish ambition or vain conceit, but in humility consider others better than your-selves. Each of you should look not only to your own interests, but also to the interests of others.

—PHILIPPIANS 2:3–4

Desire nothing for yourself, which you do not desire for others.

—BENEDICTUS DE SPINOZA

What do we make of this statement? Is this the product of poor self-esteem? Is this modesty, or worse, false modesty? Is this just a product of thinking that, to do something important in life, one must be president of the country or a chief executive officer of a Fortune 500 company? Is Rena merely a kind and altruistic person? How do we interpret the life of this woman and her contributions to better life for others? In struggling with these questions, we see some of the many paradoxes of humility.

*Rena Canipe would be genuinely embarrassed if she knew that I was writing about her. Sadly, however, her dementia will probably not permit her to appreciate that I think of her as one of my heroes of humility. Now, instead of helping others, she must be helped. She cannot remember her medications. She cannot care for her wounds when she bumps against furniture. She has to receive help, and that reality is hard for her and for her family.*

*Rena did not spend a lifetime helping others out of a sense of poor self-esteem. She knows she has helped people, yet she has not wasted her time thinking about self-importance or trying to manipulate others to admire her. She is modest but does not convey false modesty. She sees her accomplishments as important—particularly to the people*

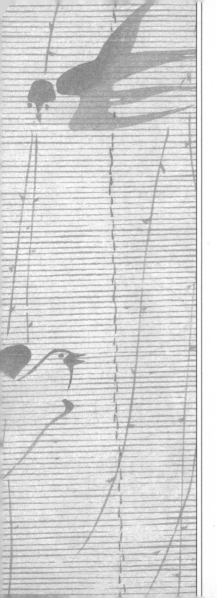

To become truly great,
one has to stand with
people, not above them.

—CHARLES DE MONTESQUIEU

It was pride that changed
angels into devils; it is
humility that makes men
as angels.

—ST. AUGUSTINE

*whose needs were being met—but not important in the grand scheme of things.*

*In this regard, she was like Mother Teresa, whom most people would place among their heroes in humility. When asked how she could possibly help all of the people in Calcutta, Mother Teresa was said to have answered, "One person at a time."*

*Rena has used her life to meet others' needs. Our lives are our greatest treasure. Rena Canipe has poured out her life as a sweet-smelling perfume. That aroma has soothed and blessed those who take it in.*

### FATHER FRANCIS CHISHOLM: LOYAL TO THE END

One of my favorite movies is *The Keys of the Kingdom,* based on a book by A. J. Cronin. The protagonist, Father Francis Chisholm, is played to perfection by Gregory Peck. The movie begins with an examiner who has come to study whether Father Chisholm should be forced to retire. The study is not encouraging. Father Francis is aging and is not seen as a stellar exemplar of a priest. He has served only one parish in China for his entire adult life.

That night, the examiner finds Father Francis' journal, and he reads the account of the priest's life. Father Francis notes no

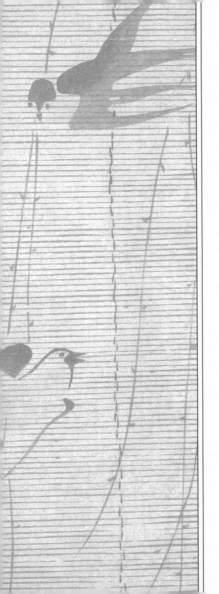

Humility is like underwear,
essential, but indecent
if it shows.

—HELEN NIELSEN

Humility, that low,
    sweet root
From which all heavenly
    virtues shoot.

—THOMAS MORE

worldly accomplishments, especially in comparison with his childhood friend, the current bishop, Anselm Mealey. Father Francis states that his ministry began in a ramshackle church in a small village in China. There were no Christians there. Eventually, one Chinese Christian walked to the village and became his lone parishioner and faithful friend.

After struggling for years with abuse from the villagers, being pelted with rotten fruit, and having no success at attracting people to his church, Father Francis is called upon one day to minister healing to the dying son of the villagers' mandarin. The dangers are enormous. If Father Francis practices westernized medicine and the boy dies, which seems likely, then his own life will be in danger. If the treatment succeeds, which seems unlikely, then it is unclear what might happen. Relying on God, Father Francis takes the risk. The young boy recovers. In gratitude, the mandarin offers to declare that he is a Christian. Father Francis declines. He insists that Christianity is believed through faith and not claimed out of obligation and gratitude. Thus, responding to the priest's authenticity, the mandarin is drawn into a relationship with Father Francis.

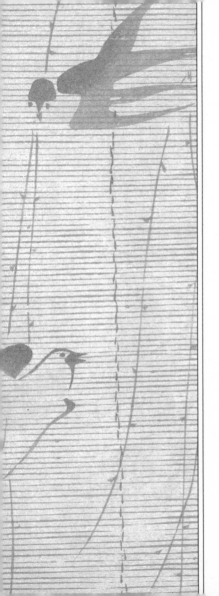

Humility is the only soil
in which the graces root.

—ANDREW MURRAY

Nuns eventually arrive to staff a village school. The Reverend Mother Maria-Veronica is a proper German Catholic, and Father Francis immediately senses her disdain. He, of course, does not engage in enough ritual and command as much authority as the reverend mother would prefer. Throughout the years, Father Francis humbly and faithfully serves the villagers, the nuns, and whoever is needy.

After many years, he is visited by his friend, Anselm Mealey, who is moving up the ecclesiastical ranks. Anselm is clearly impressed with his own importance. At first, he seems the reverend mother's ideal. Father Francis is humiliated by the accomplishments of his friend, who personally and publicly belittles Father Francis' service and modesty.

After Anselm Mealey leaves, Reverend Mother Maria-Veronica recognizes Father Francis' humility. She says,

> "This is no doubt humiliating for you. But I am obliged to tell you. I—I am sorry." The words, torn from her, gained momentum, then came in a tumbled flood. "I am most bitterly and grievously sorry for my conduct towards you. From our first meeting I have behaved

shamefully, sinfully. . . . These past ten days, in my heart, I have wept for you . . . the slights and humiliations you have endured. . . . Father, I hate myself—forgive me, forgive me. . . . If you will let me I will stay [at the mission]. I have never known anyone whom I wished so much to serve. . . . [Y]ours is the best, . . . the finest spirit I have ever known."

"Hush, my child. I am a poor and insignificant creature, . . . a common man . . . and you are a great lady. But in God's sight we are both of us children. If we may work together, . . . [we can] help each other."

Drawn to humility, the reverend mother becomes a devoted lifetime friend of Father Francis. She has been conquered by his quiet virtue.

The scene then shifts back to the examiner finishing Father Francis' diary. Having read in a night the chronicle of a humble life, the examiner reverently closes the journal.

*The Keys of the Kingdom* is fiction, but the story is repeated often around the world in many people's lives. It is about service to all people—not just ones who are similar to us. It is about loving the people whom we are given to love. It is about loyalty. It is about applying our abilities in love over a lifetime. Such love, loyalty, and universality happen in religious organizations, but they also happen in community organizations, within families, and among friends.

What do the examples of Rena Canipe and Father Francis Chisholm tell us? When they are joined with your own heroes of humility, they might reveal a consistent picture of what humility is and isn't. In the following chapter, let's examine other stories. 🌸

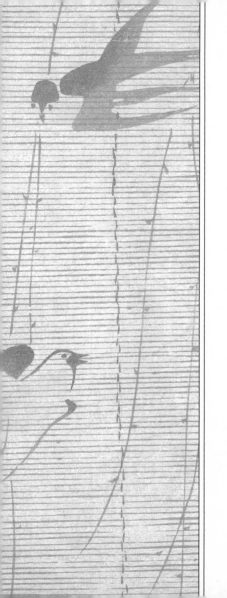

Humility is the first of virtues for other people.

—OLIVER WENDELL HOLMES

# Heroes of Humility

MOST OF US HAVE HEROES OF humility. John Seldon, a leading freedom advocate of the seventeenth century, once cynically observed, "Humility is a virtue all men preach, none practice, and yet everybody is content to hear. The master thinks it good doctrine for his servants, the laity for the clergy, and the clergy for the laity." Like Seldon, I see humility as virtuous. But I think he was wrong that "none practice" it. I believe that many people exemplify humility. And therein we will find what this paradoxical, quiet virtue of humility really is.

## JUST FOLKS

*Rena was born in 1917 as the youngest of four children to Elza Ballard Donnell, a judge in West Palm Beach, and Rena Roberts Donnell, a*

I long to accomplish a great and noble tasks, but it is my chief duty to accomplish humble tasks as though they were great and noble. The world is moved along, not only by the mighty shoves of its heroes, but also by the aggregate of the tiny pushes of each honest worker.

—HELEN KELLER

talented artist and student of Robert Henri, who, after marriage, raised her children to be fine adults. The family had its ups and downs financially. Judge Donnell would give away his last dollar to anyone in need. And because so many people knew him as a public figure, he gave away a lot of money during his life.

Rena struggled with reading, and she probably had some dyslexia that made reading a chore. Nevertheless, she graduated with honors from the University of Tennessee and went to graduate school at New York University for a master's degree in retailing. Rena's reading difficulties forced her to study hard and gave her empathy for people who had to struggle to keep their heads above water.

The work ethic taught by her mother and father and learned due to her dyslexia paid off in a teaching job at Appalachian State University. There she met Clyde Canipe, the eldest son of a pastor. Clyde was forced to take over as head of the home when his father died of pneumonia when the boy was ten.

Rena and Clyde married and started a family just before World War II broke out. Clyde was drafted into the Army Air Corps. The early years of marriage were difficult for the Canipes. They struggled financially. But the values of the Donnells and the working-class work ethic of the Canipes melded into a strong family, centered around the children

The insignificances of daily life are the importances and the tests of eternity, because they prove what really is the spirit that possesses us. It is our most unguarded moments that we really show and see what we are. To know the humble man, . . . you must follow him in the common course of daily life.

**—ANDREW MURRAY**

*and supported by Clyde's salary as a teacher and sports coach. It was a humble start to this family.*

Obviously, Rena Canipe is my first hero of humility. My second is Arthur Reppert, a member of a small church that I have attended for the last thirty years, Christ Presbyterian Church in Richmond, Virginia. Arthur has served the church as a deacon, seeking to dispense charity to the people who are needy and come to church for help. He has also served as an elder on the Session, which is responsible for the operation of the church. Arthur has been involved in Prison Fellowship. The ministry was founded by Chuck Colson, a former advisor to President Richard Nixon, who spent time in prison after the Watergate scandal. Arthur has helped prisoners and former prisoners for many years. He and his wife Joan have invited former prisoners, pregnant girls, and homeless people to live in their home. Arthur and Joan have served countless needy people with dedication.

Arthur has a quirky sense of humor. He can tease and laugh openly. He can be tough when he needs to be tough and tender when he needs to be tender. As far as I know, Arthur has never won an award for his unselfish and humble service. Unless such

No labor, however humble,

is dishonoring.

—THE TALMUD

an award was given in my presence, I probably would not know about it. Arthur doesn't flaunt awards and recognition. He simply keeps his head down and serves people who need help.

My third hero of humility is Kathy Ingram, a psychology professor at Virginia Commonwealth University. Although many faculty members have a heart for students, Kathy may be the one who gives the most dedicated service to students and other faculty. She does an enormous amount of work, yet she does not complain. She is eager to help others.

## ESTEEMED PROFESSIONALS

Rena, Arthur, and Kathy have not been recognized nationally or internationally for exemplary accomplishments, yet they are in my Hall of Humility. I also know several people who have received the highest levels of accolades for achievement: They too are extremely humble.

One of these is Russell Stannard. Trained as a physicist, Russell was a faculty member at the Free University in England. He has appeared on BBC television many times as a science educator. He truly loves science, and he seeks to give that love away to millions of children. He has written a series of popular

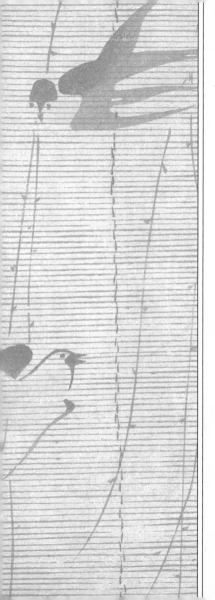

I have done one braver thing
Than all the Worthies did,
And yet a braver thence
   did spring,
Which is to keep that hid.

—JOHN DONNE

Do good by stealth,
and blush to find it fame.

—ALEXANDER POPE

True merit, like a river,
the deeper it is, the less
noise it makes.

—EDWARD FREDERICK HALIFAX

children's books on science (the "Uncle Albert" series) and on how scientific concepts can be explained simply. He is an excellent science writer for adults as well. When I talk with Russell, I have to pry his accomplishments out of him. He is a loving person who would rather talk about science than about his honors. I knew Russell for ten years before I found that he also was an accomplished sculptor.

Yet another hero in humility is psychologist David Myers. Dave is an excellent social scientist, writer, and speaker. His real contribution has been to write the best-selling introductory psychology textbook. Through this book, Dave has made a lot of money. However, he has given most of this money away through private foundations. This is not something that everyone knows, because Dave and his wife have humble spirits and do not share their commitment to philanthropy widely.

These heroes in my Hall of Humility are role models for me and for many of the people who know them. They embody the spirit of humility. Perhaps they do not believe that they are making a difference, but they are. They surely do not shout their accomplishments, yet the lives they touch are elevated. They are ambassadors of virtue and character. They inspire me.

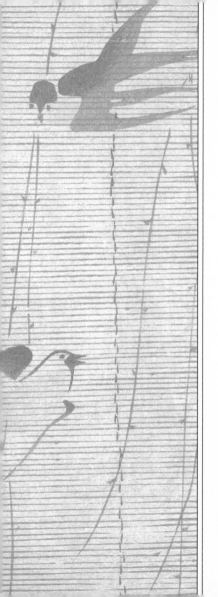

The most powerful weapon to conquer evil is humility. For evil does not know at all how to employ it, nor does it know how to defend itself against it.

—ST. VINCENT DE PAUL

A beautiful story of humility, *The Fourth Wise Man,* is based on Henry van Dyke's novella *The Story of the Other Wise Man.* In the film version, Martin Sheen portrays a rich man named Artaban—one of four magi (wise men)—who longs to be present at the birth of the Christ child. While he is converting his entire fortune into three precious jewels, the other three wise men set out by camel to follow the star that would eventually lead them to Bethlehem.

Artaban, accompanied by a whiny attendant (played by Alan Arkin), sells one of his three jewels to purchase what is needed to make the journey. Coming to Bethlehem as Herod's troops are killing Jewish children, he purchases the life of one child with the second of his three jewels.

Artaban and his attendant next stumble into a leper colony. The fourth wise man agrees to stay, using his medical training to help the lepers "just for one day." One day turns to two, which turn to years. Still, Artaban hopes someday to see Jesus to give him the final jewel.

When the existence of the leper colony is threatened, Artaban offers to trade his final jewel for seeds that could yield

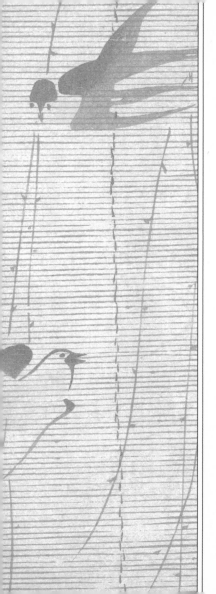

Without humility there can be no humanity.

—JOHN BUCHAN

The person who renders loyal service in a humble capacity will be chosen for higher responsibilities, just as the biblical servant who multiplied the one given him by his master was made ruler over ten cities.

—B. C. FORBES

crops to sustain the colony, but his friends refuse his sacrifice. Later, the final jewel is put to use when he purchases freedom from slavery for a friend's daughter. Thirty years from the story's start, the fourth wise man has spent his fortune, and his health, on others.

One day, word arrives: Jesus has come to Jerusalem. A blind friend of Artaban has been healed. "Come. Let's go see him," says the friend.

In the most poignant moment of the film, the fourth wise man looks at his destitute surroundings, feels his weak, work-worn heart, and—after having poured out his life for others—says plainly, "But I have nothing to give him."

### A PERSONAL EXPERIENCE

Probably like you, I know enough about my own heart and its self-centered motives not to think of myself as humble. But I have had some moments—all too rare—of humility. Perhaps the one I recall most often occurred after my mother was beaten to death by a youthful home invader seeking treasures.

The first day after the murder, hatred engulfed me as we tried to sort out the events. It was not until about 3 a.m. that I

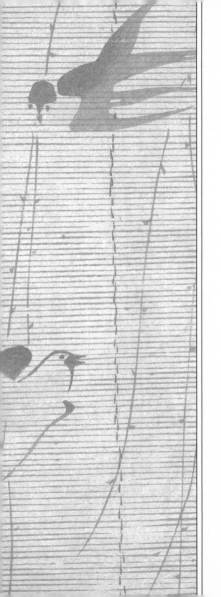

I will study and get ready
and someday my chance
will come.

**—ABRAHAM LINCOLN**

even thought the word *forgiveness*. As a researcher who studied forgiveness, a therapist who encouraged it, a speaker who spoke often about it, and a writer who had less than a month before I delivered a book manuscript to my publisher on forgiveness, it seems logical to me (looking back) that I would think early and often about the possibility of forgiving the murder. But all that day, I had treated forgiveness as the f-word.

Late at night, amid my solitary, rage-fueled pacing, I finally thought through what the murder must have been like from the young murderer's point of view. I empathized with the youth. I could understand that he might feel that his freedom would end because Mama had seen him while committing burglary. I could see how a youth who already had an impulse-control problem might hastily lash out with the crowbar in frustration that his perfect crime had been spoiled.

As I pictured him striking my mom with the crowbar, my mind flashed back to hours earlier. I had stood in my brother Mike's back room, pointed to a baseball bat, and said, "I wish that whoever did this were here. I would beat his brains out."

I had just imagined the scene of gory violence and pain: a youth beating my mother with a crowbar. When I remembered how I had wished to kill him with the baseball bat, I knew I had myself done wrong. True, I had not acted violently as he had. But what if he had stood in front of me during my rage? I might have killed him.

The sad truth was that I had uncovered bloodlust in my heart. I saw that I was no better than the murderer. Aleksandr Solzhenitsyn once wrote, "If only there were evil people somewhere insidiously committing evil deeds, and it were necessary only to separate them from the rest of us and destroy them. But the line dividing good and evil cuts through the heart of every human being. And who is willing to destroy a piece of his own heart?"

In fact, in some ways, I knew I was even worse than the youth. His plans to quick riches had been suddenly interrupted by my mother's appearance. His response was knee-jerk. Yet I had suckled my hatred on a seven-hour trip from Richmond, Virginia, to Knoxville, Tennessee; nurtured it all day as the detectives unfolded the story of the murder; and pampered it by plotting murder in my vengeful heart. I had thought for hours about his violence. I could not plead impulsiveness, yet I was willing to kill him.

I felt embarrassed, ashamed, and guilty. That guilt was compounded because I'm a Christian. Yet I could truly sense my kinship with the youthful murderer. We were blood brothers. I desired, within the core of my heart, to murder.

When we are wronged, it is easy to feel morally superior. It is easier to condemn someone who is different from me than it is to condemn someone who is similar to me. That is why warring enemies emphasize their differences. That is why we dehumanize people whom we wish to hurt. We say they are animals, vermin. We want to exact revenge without seeing their similarity to us. As I saw my own vengeful heart, though, I experienced a moment of humility. I could not feel superior to the youth.

My guilt immediately triggered the Christian thoughts that I had practiced for years. When we truly feel guilty, rather than condemn ourselves, we can take our guilt to God. God will forgive. God's love and mercy are the basis of forgiveness. Like Christians worldwide and throughout history, I knew that I could confess my wrongdoing with sincere regret. God is kind and would forgive.

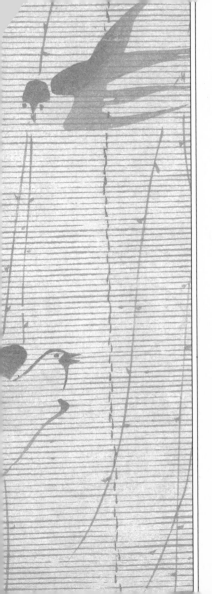

True love is the parent
of humility.

—WILLIAM ELLERY CHANNING

The only wisdom
we can hope to acquire
is the wisdom
of humility.
Humility is endless.

—T. S. ELIOT

I *could* confess. But *would* I? Sensing our own guilt can shame us. Shame makes us want to hide our sin. Our life is like a fruit-laden tree, covered with good and bad fruit. We often pluck the low-hanging, easy-to-see bad fruit and bury it where we think no one will see it. Yet we know what will happen in due season. The rotten fruit we buried will burst from the ground as fruit trees, and each will produce bushels of bad fruit. Instead, we should gather all the bad fruit we can—the easy-to-see bad fruit and that fruit hidden behind healthy-looking leaves. Then we must take the fruit to God, who will burn it up. Our fruit trees will then be cleansed of bad fruit.

So I prayed to be forgiven for my darkened heart and bloodlust toward the youth. I felt God's forgiveness for my hatred and the murderous intent within me. When that happened, I was flooded with gratitude toward a merciful and loving God. It made me want to give something precious to the youth because I had been given something precious. I gave forgiveness. In my life, there are too few moments of humility. But that was one.

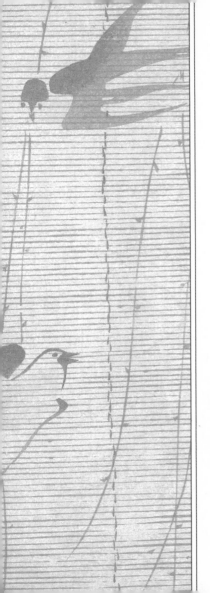

Love is hoarded

Molds at last

Until we know someday

The only thing

We ever have

Is what we give away.

**—EDNA ST. VINCENT MILLAY**

# What Do These Heroes
# Have in Common?

I SEE HUMILITY—AMONG THE many characteristics it quietly reveals—as necessarily involving serving others. William Temple wrote, "Humility does not mean thinking less of yourself than of other people, nor does it mean having a low opinion of your own gifts. It means freedom from thinking about yourself at all." Humility is not letting our minds go blank. Instead, our minds are focused. But instead of focusing on ourselves, we try to discern others' needs. We empathize with them. We sympathize. We feel compassion. We feel and show love for the people who come across our path. And we loyally yield to virtue.

## HUMILITY IS NOT THE SAME THING AS ALTRUISM

Humility, though, is not merely another word for altruism. People can be altruistic for egoistical motives. They can serve

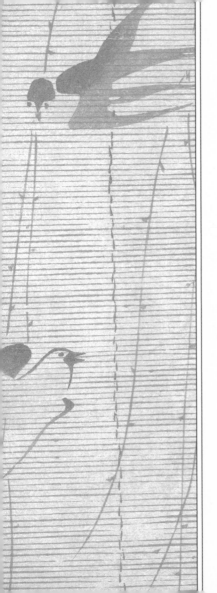

The praise that comes from love does not make us vain, but more humble.

—SIR JAMES M. BARRIE

You shouldn't gloat about anything you've done; you ought to keep going and find something better to do.

—DAVID PACKARD

others because they get rewarded for serving. They may seek honor, recognition, awards, a helper's exhilaration, or relief from guilt or helplessness. Egoistic altruists act altruistically. This altruism is virtuous. It is an excellent human quality to aspire to.

But humility is more than altruism done primarily for self-interested motives. Certainly, good feelings arise when anyone helps another person. Yet for the humble person, good feelings and rewards are unsought by-products, not motivations. His or her motivation is seeing needs, feeling positive emotions toward the needy person, and then acting to meet those needs *so that* the other person experiences less suffering or more happiness and well-being in life.

## HUMILITY CAN BE SEEN IN AN ACT OF GOODNESS, A SEASON OF LIFE, OR A LIFETIME OF VIRTUE

Humility can be a single act. A person who is self-absorbed can be moved to compassion and can act humbly in a moment. Humility might also characterize a season in some people's lives. They carry out many acts of humble service. For the rare person—like Rena Canipe—humility is a character trait, a way of life. Of course, these people may have moments of pride. They

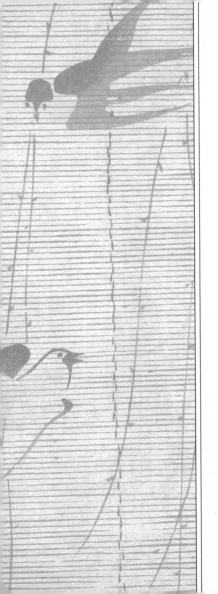

Earnestness is not by any means everything; it is very often a subtle form of pious pride because it is obsessed with the method and not with the master.

—OSWALD CHAMBERS

may have times when they grit their teeth and serve from a sense of duty or conscientiousness. But mostly their lives are driven by a desire to help and bless other people, to remove or reduce suffering in the world every way that they can. They see something in this life that is bigger than they are.

## PART OF HUMILITY IS SEEING AND HONORING SOMETHING BIGGER THAN I AM

We see ourselves as creature and God as Creator. The Hindu mystic Sri Ramakrishna Paramahamsa said, "Great sages have childlike natures. Before God they are always like children. They have no pride. Their strength is the strength of God, the strength of their Father. They have nothing to call their own. They are firmly convinced of that."

We also stand in humility when we see our place within humanity. Chief Seattle, chief of the Suquamish and Duwamish Native American tribes in the Pacific Northwest, said, "Man does not weave this web of life. He is merely a strand of it. Whatever he does to the web, he does to himself."

We also stand in humility as we see our relationship to the environment. Environmental activist Rachel Carson, author of

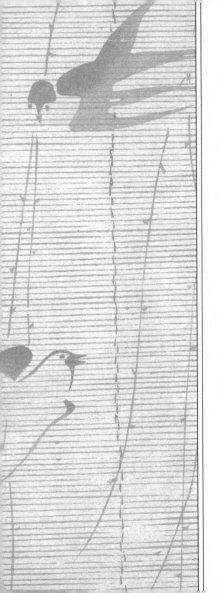

It is unwise to be too sure of one's own wisdom. It is healthy to be reminded that the strongest might weaken and the wisest might err.

—MOHANDAS K. GANDHI

the classic and still influential book *Silent Spring,* said, "It is a wholesome and necessary thing for us to turn again to the earth and in the contemplation of her beauties to know of wonder and humanity."

Moving our vision wider, we stand in humility when we see our life in relationship to the cosmos. Cultural anthropologist and humanitarian Joseph Campbell said, "The goal of life is to make your heartbeat match the beat of the universe, to match your nature with Nature."

In humility, we find something bigger than we are. The bigger—God, humanity, the environment, or the cosmos—differs across people, communities, and cultures. But the constant in the equation is this. Something is bigger than we are. And we know it. Science shows how much we focus on our own self-serving biases, as we will see in a later chapter. These biases are hard to overcome.

## HUMILITY IS FREEDOM FROM HAVING TO FOCUS ON THE SELF

William Temple's quote captures humility for me: "Humility . . . means freedom from thinking about yourself at all." Most heroes

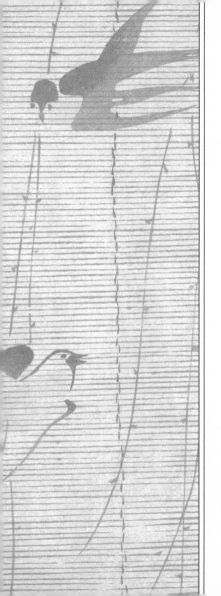

Humility leads to strength
and not to weakness.
It is the highest form
of self-respect to admit
mistakes and to make
amends for them.

—JOHN (JAY) McCLOY

of humility share an attitude that has become a personality characteristic—thinking first of God, nature, the environment, or the cosmos, they turn their attention to need. That need resides in the suffering and privation of others. Thus, the humble person is unshackled from an inner self-serving drive and is energized by laying his or her own fettering interests aside and making others' interests (while still preserving one's integrity and not being a doormat) worthy of pursuing.

We see this clearly in the founders of the world's great religions. Moses was a humble leader, yet he saw God's face. Jesus continually directed people to God the Father, and in doing so, changed the balance of power from Rome to Christendom in the centuries following his life on earth. Muhammad was a strong leader who sought obedience to God above all virtues. Gandhi's humility undid the power of England, the strongest nation on earth during his lifetime. Siddhartha founded a new religion by finding humility and losing his self. People followed these religious leaders partly because they spoke with a ring of truth and integrity but partly also because they humbly gave their live in the service of others without drawing focus to themselves.

Religion is to do right.
It is to love, it is to think,
it is to be humble.

—RALPH WALDO EMERSON

## SERVING OTHERS

*Rena Canipe had four daughters and two sons, though the eldest son drowned at one and one-half years old. With the girls, Rena threw herself into the Girl Scouts as a leader and volunteer. Over the years, she felt that the religious aspect of scouting was being systematically de-emphasized. She worked to prevent its elimination altogether. So, in her honor, a religious award was established. Girl Scouting encourages girls to grow strong in faith. Girl Scouting recognizes that religious instruction must come from families and faith communities rather than from the leader of the scouts. Thus, the religious award is administered by the girl's own faith tradition. In 2000, Rena was honored by the Girl Scouts of America with her picture in its calendar for her sustained service, especially in humbly pointing girls toward God to temper the girls' pride of their just accomplishments.*

## OTHERS' OPINIONS REVEAL HUMILITY

True humility, as revealed by examining heroes of humility, meets others' needs. It thus is noticed by others more than by oneself. The humble have reason to boast (at least in the eyes of others) but do not do so. They refrain from boasting not because of suppression of strong internal drives to brag. They do not

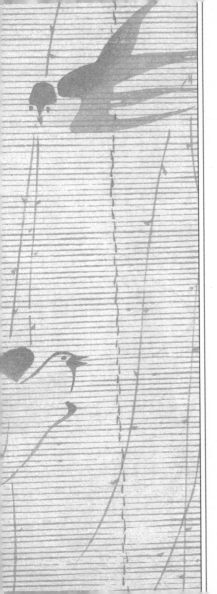

Humility comes
from understanding
that the obstacles
in front of you are not
going to go away.

—SARAH FERGUSON


Do you wish to rise?
Begin by descending.
You plan a tower
that will pierce the clouds?
Lay first the foundation
of humility.

—ST. AUGUSTINE

refrain because they hope that a false modesty will attract attention. Rather, they do not boast because they are secure enough in their identity that building themselves up in the eyes of the world is unimportant. Also, they are busy thinking of others. Their humility is a character trait of seeing themselves in proper perspective against bigger and grander things.

One paradox of humility, then, is that others' evaluations count more than one's own self-evaluation in identifying humility. Self-evaluation does matter. Humility is a virtue, and many people desire to act virtuously. If people aspire to virtue (and clearly not all people do), then how do we reach humility?

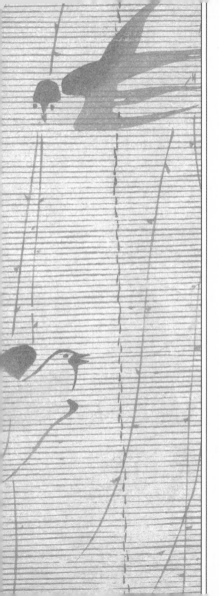

This is the true self-denial
to which our Savior calls us,
the acknowledgement that
self has nothing good in it,
except as an empty vessel
which God must fill.

—ANDREW MURRAY

# Can We Learn Humility?

WE CAN SEE THAT MANY PEOPLE value humility. We also see that it is complex. So, now is the perfect time to introduce my program for the five steps downward into the glory of humble service. I confess. I don't have such a program. Moreover, think of this. Perhaps no such program is possible.

Perhaps humility is not something we can systematically learn in some five-step program. Perhaps the opposite of humility—self-focus—simply is too ingrained in our nature. Oliver Wendell Holmes observed, "Most of us retain enough of the theological attitude to think that we are little gods." In our better moments, we see how ugly we make ourselves when we enthrone ourselves on tiny thrones and crown ourselves with paper crowns. Yet we persist in making ourselves American idols, singing our own praises. On the other hand, there is something within us that chastises our folly. The reality television phenomenon *American Idol* employs a panel of critics to critique singers who aspired to be American idols. One judge in particular, Simon Cowell, has been likely to deliver corrective feedback. We have within us a voice that tells us that singing our own praise is always out of tune. Usually our own praise song is sharp—at least a half tone too high.

This does not mean that people have not created step-by-step guides to humility. For example, in chapter 7 of *The Rule of St. Benedict,* Benedict prescribes disciplines of humility for monks. The monk ascends the ladder of humility degree by degree for twelve degrees. The twelve disciplines do not themselves make the monk humble; they merely provide the outward form into which God can pour humility. Therefore, to have God make the monk humble, the monk

1. always has the fear of God before his eyes.
2. loves God's will more than his own.
3. subjects himself obediently to a superior.
4. accepts distasteful duties with patience.

5. confesses his failures completely.
6. is content with little.
7. believes and declares to others that he has no worth apart from God.
8. does nothing that is not approved by the religious community.
9. disciplines himself through silence.
10. is restrained in demeanor.
11. engages only in sober talk.
12. is not only humble of heart, but lets others know he is sinful.

In the eleventh century, Bernard of Clairvaux wrote an expanded commentary on Benedict's twelve steps upward into humility and then wrote on the twelve steps downward into pride. Over the years, others have tried their hands at the same topic, but no program seems to have taken hold universally. While there is no agreed-upon program to produce humility, there are actions we can take. Over thirty years ago, I heard a speaker quote a brief poem that captures our struggle as humans.

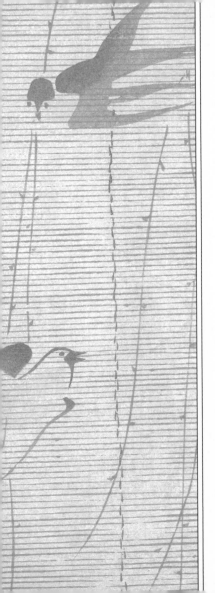

O Lord,
Remember not only the men
and women of good will but
all those of ill will. But do not
remember all the suffering
they have inflicted upon us;
remember the fruits we
have bought thanks to this
suffering—our comradeship,
our loyalty, our humility,
our courage, our generosity,
the greatness of heart which
has grown out of all this;
and when they come to judg-
ment, let all the fruits we have
borne be their forgiveness.

**—FOUND IN THE RAVENSBRUCK
CONCENTRATION CAMP**

*Two natures beat within my breast.*
*One is cursed; one is blessed.*
*One I love; one I hate.*
*The one I feed will dominate.*

To walk toward humility, I must starve the arrogant nature and feed the humble nature. Try as I might, I cannot kill either. But I can do my part to allow humility to reveal itself.

## NEGATE THE NEGATIVE

*Nix narcissism.* Narcissism is an exclusive focus on the self. The narcissist holds a grandiose and inflated sense of self. In Greek mythology, Narcissus fell in love with his own reflection. Humility at a bare minimum recognizes that life is not "all about me." The focus is appropriately on others—but on others' needs, not others' misdeeds.

*Eliminate entitlement.* Entitled people believe that they are superior to others in a way that qualifies them for special treatment. Thus, they are often preoccupied with fairness as they perceive it. When people are both narcissistic and entitled, they perceive themselves to be unique, special, and deserving in ways

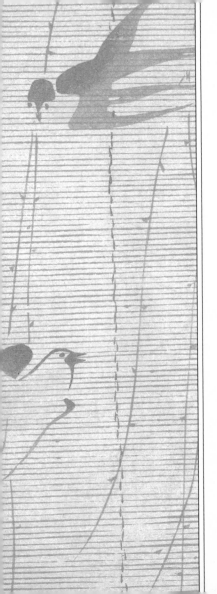

There ain't never a horse
that's never been rode;
there ain't never a rider
that can't be thrown.

—GARY COOPER

Life is a long lesson
of humility.

—JAMES M. BARRIE

A traveler am I and a
navigator, and every day
I discover a new region
within my soul.

—KAHLIL GIBRAN

that other people are not. Thus, entitled narcissists usually blame others for misunderstandings, are easily offended, often feel unappreciated, believe that others owe them and that the debt owed is disproportionately large. They are usually highly motivated to redress perceived injustices through seeking restitution or revenge. They are unwilling to cancel debts or forgive and forget unless the offender pays back virtually all of the debt that is owed (with interest). Even then, forgiveness is expected to be met with effusive gratitude.

True humility puts aside both narcissism and its entitlement subtheme. Humble people tend not to point to others or to themselves when things go wrong. They fix problems, not assign blame. Although they might have a strong sense of justice, they tend to be defenders of the needy, not vigilantes who patrol their relationships looking for ways to accuse or punish wrongdoers.

*Puncture pride.* Pride puffs up. We probably all feel pride, and sometimes our pride is justly deserved. At other times, pride is a defensive shield to protect a fragile ego. Bishop Fulton Sheen said, "Pride is an admission of weakness; it secretly fears all competition and dreads all rivals." I don't like to feel prideful. Perhaps

"Pride goes before destruction; a haughty spirit before a fall" (Prov. 16:18) has become such a part of our culture that the feeling of swelling up is thought to be anything but swell. Few people have described the problem so clearly and succinctly as Benjamin Franklin. He noted, "Pride that dines on vanity sups on contempt." Feeling good about ourselves, we often may devalue others.

Whenever I begin to feel prideful, I use a vivid story to deflate my swollen head. Unfortunately, I have forgotten the source of the story.

A college man was lifting weights. He stole frequent side-long glances at the mirror to note his bulging muscles. *Watch out, Arnold Schwarzenegger,* he thought. *I'll go to the Commons to give the women a treat.* (Did I mention that humility was not his strong suit?) Slipping his sleeveless tank top over his naked torso (and flexing a couple of times), he glanced again at the mirror. Thinking that the scholar athlete would be more impressive than the mere athlete, he blew the dust off of a few textbooks and tucked the six weightiest under his arm. *I'll be a legend in my own time,* he thought.

At the Commons, he bought college health food: burger, fries, and shake. Balancing the tray with one hand and his books with the other, he swaggered toward a seat. Instinctively, he knew that every woman was looking at him lustfully.

He caught the eyes of a cluster of gorgeous women. He casually leaned down to drink from his straw. Missed. Embarrassed, he lunged at the straw again. It bounced off of his lip. His straining lips and thrusting tongue chased that pesky straw in NASCAR-like laps around the cup, but it eluded him like a rolling stone. *Not cool.* Finally, he lurched at the straw. It bounced off of his lip and lodged in his right nostril. *Definitely not cool.* He flexed his nose. The straw hung there. He shook his head and twitched his lips grotesquely. He sniffed. *Bad idea.* He blew. Okay, you're seeing his intellectual prowess in full flower. Bubbles splattered the milkshake onto his face. In desperation, he jerked his head backwards. But the straw came with him. He suddenly became the-amazing-jerk-with-the-straw-in-his-snoz—an instant legend in his own time, just as he predicted. Swinging his head from side to side, he did a Jackson Pollack-like milkshake-splatter painting of nearby people. He was a popular guy, all right, and the talk of campus for about a week.

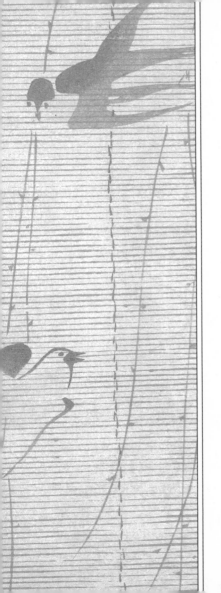

The strongest poison
ever known
Came from Caesar's
laurel crown.

—WILLIAM BLAKE

Recalling that story can snap me out of any "he's-a-legend-in-his-own-mind" mood. Overweening pride is ugly. As Lincoln once said, "What kills a skunk is the publicity it gives itself." Journalist and public commentator Gilbert K. Chesterton once said, "If I had only one sermon to preach, it would be a sermon against pride."

Yet, developing humility is more than merely defeating pride—though that is part of it. Humility involves other internal and external qualities. It involves modesty and honest self-appraisal. It is not a mere product of poor self-esteem. It is thinking of the other person empathically and lovingly.

*Equalize egoism with empathy.* How can we keep the focus off ourselves? It is not by commanding "Do not think of yourself." Harvard psychologist Daniel Wegner has studied how unsuccessful we can be at suppressing unwanted thoughts. He instructed undergraduates, "Don't think about white bears. In fact, as an experiment, try this right now. Do not think about white bears. Don't think about the color of their fur or the shape of their nose. Don't think about the scratch-scratch of their claws on the snow. Absolutely do not try to recall the shape of their ears or imagine what their breath might smell like."

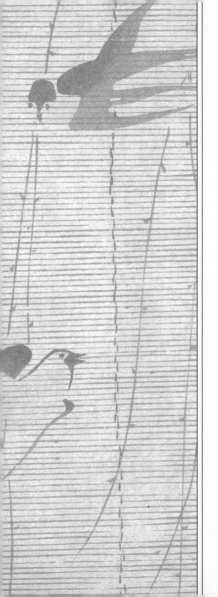

In general, pride is at the bottom of all great mistakes.

**—JOHN RUSKIN**

Once the game is over,
the king and the pawn
go back in the same box.

**—ITALIAN PROVERB**

If you played along with Wegner, how did you do in thinking about white beans? If you are like most people, you thought about, and kept thinking about them. Why? Because we cannot suppress thoughts effectively. At best, we might distract ourselves so that we thought about dark bears or sunny beaches.

Similarly, I cannot become more humble by trying to not focus on myself. I'm caught in the white-bear paradox.

What if we think instead about others? How might he be feeling right now? What might she be thinking or doing? What did he imagine that might have made him so grumpy? What was going on with my boss when she was short with me?

There. I'll bet you didn't think about white bears. You were too busy thinking of other people, their thoughts, feelings, needs, and personal experiences. Not focusing on oneself is helped by having something worthy to think about. Often that is the needy other person.

## CULTIVATE AN ACCURATE SENSE OF SELF

*Secure self-confidence and self-esteem—but not too much.* Poor self-esteem can motivate people to serve others altruistically and to avoid attention modestly. When you feel like a worm, you can

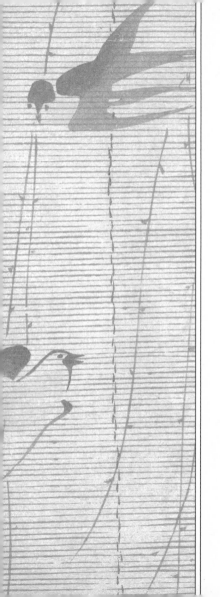

By these things examine thyself. By whose rules am I acting; in whose name; in whose strength; in whose glory? What faith, humility, self-denial, and love of God and of man have there been in all my actions?

—JACKIE MASON

wiggle ingratiatingly to avoid being stepped on. Lack of self-worth, however, is not humility, though it might be mistaken for it by those who don't know us. Poor self-esteem is focused intently on the self. It is aimed at self-protection.

Paradoxically, high self-esteem can also result in the same behaviors. When people hold themselves in high regard but their self-esteem is fragile, they will decisively stamp out any challenge to their seeming self-confidence. A person can appear to have all of his ducks in a row until a challenge blasts them like a shotgun.

Self-confidence allows people freedom from fear, which permits humble service. Christian writer Oswald Chambers said, "Self-confidence is either petty pride in our own narrowness or the realization of our duty and privilege as God's children." Self-confidence walks a knife-edge that cuts through the heart of humans as do good and evil.

*Be self-aware, but not too self-aware.* Sometimes humility is hampered, and sometimes aided, by simple self-awareness. Some people seem to be attuned to their own inner lives and to how others perceive them. In humility, they may wage a lifelong battle against pride, made more difficult by their self-awareness.

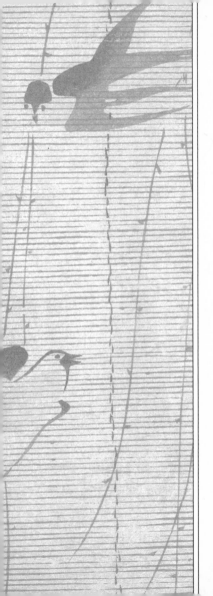

The first test of a truly
great man is his humility.
By humility I don't mean
doubt of power or hesitation
in speaking his opinion,
but merely an understanding
of the relationship of what
he can say and what he
can do.

—JOHN RUSKIN

They are overalert to the ways life affects them, too self-aware. In their thought-life, they see themselves as a bright sun at their center and see others as the orbiting lesser lights. Benjamin Franklin said, "A man wrapped up in himself makes a small bundle."

Others are just not very self-aware at all. This isn't an earned virtue but a blessing of inheritance. Some people look not inward but outward at others, not for others' reactions to them but for others' sake. They see events "out there," and those events capture their attention. Like so many of the virtues, self-awareness is both a blessing and a curse. We can err through being too self-aware or not self-aware enough.

## LEAP FROM THE LIMELIGHT

Modesty is the avoidance of attention to oneself. We often equate modesty with humility, and sometimes the two do go together. However, modesty can arise not only from humility but from discomfort over our looks, poor self-confidence, having been previously ridiculed in a similar situation, simple parental admonitions to be modest, or group pressure to act modestly. Modesty is more winsome than pride, yet it is not to

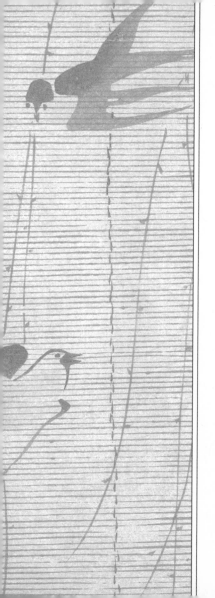

Lord, where we are wrong,

make us willing to change;

where we are right,

make us easy to live with.

—PETER MARSHALL

be equated with humility. Worse, we all are egoistic at times. Laurence J. Peter, educator and best known for elucidating the "Peter Principle," observed, "There are two kinds of egoists: those who admit it, and the rest of us."

False modesty appears at first blush to be modesty. It is the finger that points ostentatiously to give credit to another person or to God, while the other three fingers—partially obscured by the thumb—point back at ourselves. The purpose of false modesty is to elicit a double recognition. It calls attention to the self for doing or being something wonderful, and through saying "Aw, shucks," it calls attention to the self for modesty. Is it any wonder that Thomas Fuller, a British historian, said, "Pride, perceiving humility honorable, often borrows her cloak."

## LIVE VIRTUOUSLY

*Practice virtues.* Virtue is what is good. Psychologist Martin Seligman suggests that people can pursue *the happy life,* which is focused on their own pleasure; *the good life,* which benefits self and others; or *the meaningful life,* which gives a noble purpose to self and others. What is virtuous is understood within context. The scope of our context—focus on self; on self and others;

or on self, others, and noble purpose—determines the virtues we pursue.

When we look at others who are humble, we usually say that they seem to be living the meaningful life. And humble people feel, at least in their better moments, that they have pursued something meaningful.

*Cultivate religion or spirituality.* Spirituality is one's personal search for the sacred. Religion is that search within a community that holds agreed-upon beliefs, values, and practices. The sacred is something greater than the self. Humble people often feel that they are responding to a calling from beyond themselves.

## WHY IS BEING HUMBLE SUCH A STRUGGLE?

Humility, if pursued intentionally, is difficult. It requires negating the negative, seeing the self in true perspective, being modest, and pursuing noble purpose. These four steps are like climbing a mountain.

*Self-serving bias.* Cognitive science has shown repeatedly that people's mental lives are characterized by a self-serving bias. People desire predictability and stability. Surviving and flourishing depend on being able to predict the future accurately so one can order one's life. Usually, it is to our advantage to generalize from our observations throughout life and make rules, or heuristics, that capture the way things seem to be. These heuristics help people make quick decisions that are correct or wise most of the time without going through painful considerations of every possible alternative behavior, every choice.

Our personalities are in many ways sets of these generalizations about life. A person who believes his or her signature strength to be loyalty will usually act loyally. A person who is forgiving will generally forgive more readily than a vengeful person. A humble person tends to have a general rule that humble attitudes and behavior are helpful in negotiating life. A person who is narcissistic or entitled believes the opposite—that people will treat the narcissist as special. That rule helps the person negotiate life, though it often leaves a trail of damaged relationships in its wake.

*Human limitation.* Living humbly is hard. Besides the need for stability that leads to a natural self-serving bias (which points us away from humility), we also simply are imperfect and

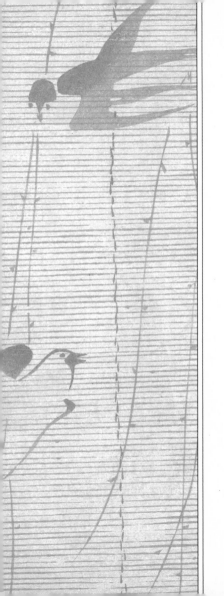

Blushing is the color
of virtue.

—DIOGENES

frequently fail morally to live up to our own standards. Such imperfections and failures are challenging. They threaten self-esteem. Any cracks in our sense of self-worth are magnified like a fissure along a fault line in the tremors that occur when misfortune and challenge rock our world. We defend ourselves instinctively. Thus, it is hard to maintain humility in the face of our all-too-real limitations.

One of my great adventures with my two oldest children was hiking Mount Washington. Christen was nine and Jonathan, seven. Mount Washington leaps vertically straight up for four thousand feet. The climb is mercilessly unrelenting. After a final, long rock scramble, we reached the summit. Our reward was whipping forty-mile-per-hour wind and impenetrable mist. On the way to the top, the views from some of the plateaus were spectacular. The thrill of walking a six-inch ledge over wet stones and looking into a one-thousand-foot-deep basin was both terrifying and exhilarating. Although the summit was initially disappointing, Christen, Jonathan, and I huddled in the lee of the summit and ate our mustard sandwiches. (Yes, I forgot to include the meat.) Despite all the hardships, we have hardly ever felt so gratified.

Self-conceit shows a lack
of sensibility and maturity.
Those who are more
reflective and spiritually
mature have the sense to
attribute whatever gifts they
may have to the Creator,
the Most High, and devote
themselves to him with
humble gratitude.

**—M. FETHULLA GULEN**

Putting aside the exalted self in pursuit of modesty and virtue as we subdue self-serving bias is similar to climbing a moral Mount Washington. The view from our destination is not always what we expected. Sometimes we even eat mustard sandwiches. But in humble service, we rest in gratification.

## SOMETIMES LIFE INTRUDES

*Rena was always exceptionally active. I remember when she decided to enter the Golden Olympics. Although she was an avid tennis player, at age sixty-five, she had never run distances. So she turned her self-discipline toward running. On the day of the race, one mile from the venue, her tire blew. Undaunted, she leapt from the car and began to run.*

*She arrived at the registration table as the contestants lurched forward at the bang of the starter's pistol. Quickly, she registered, grabbed her number, and sprinted past the starting line. Not only did she win the sixty-five-and-over competition, but her time was better than the sixty-and-over winner.*

*Even in her eighties, Rena rode her bike all over the West Palm Beach area. One day, at age eighty-two, after a ten-mile ride, she arrived home dehydrated. Her foot caught as she dismounted. Like a slow-motion movie, she hopped, fell, and saw the pavement rush toward her. Darkness.*

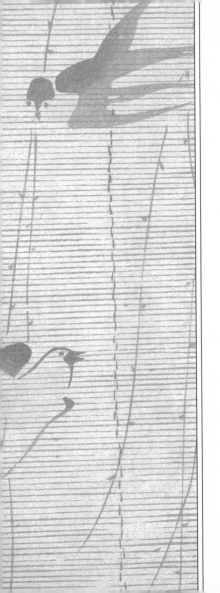

Keep me away from the wisdom which does not cry, the philosophy which does not laugh, and the greatness which does not bow before children.

—KAHLIL GIBRAN

*Rena sustained a brain injury from striking her head on the concrete. As so often is the case when head injuries occur in the elderly, she began to forget things. Just names, dates, faces, details at first. Then current events. Confusion happened. It was worse as she moved from her home of fifty years in Lake Park to Jupiter, ten miles away.*

*As Rena lost mental functions, the family became more concerned. Tensions arose over decisions about the best way to love and care for her. It is a story that is repeated in too many families these days. And with the Baby Boomer population aging, the story is expected to become even more common.*

"How do we love Mama, respect her life, and honor her even as her sense of identity is visibly slipping away daily?" With Rena, this question was particularly difficult. Much of her identity was wrapped up in being a helper. Now, not only could she rarely help anyone, but her frail body and mind were ever-present reminders that she was losing who she was. 🏵

I prefer to be a dreamer
among the humblest,
with visions to be realized,
than lord among those
without dreams
and desires.

**—KAHLIL GIBRAN**

# What Does Science Tell Us about Humility?

SCIENCE TELLS US PRECIOUS LITTLE about humility. Only a few scientists have attempted to measure and write scientifically about the quiet virtue. I want to tell you what they have found, but to avoid bogging down the book with "science-talk," I'll describe the essence of the findings and provide the scientific references at the end of the book for those interested in learning more.

## THE DIFFICULTY IN MEASURING HUMILITY

In 2000, June Tangney, a professor at George Mason University, pointed out how difficult it is to measure humility using self-report questionnaires. Tangney argued that, if humility really involves the forgetting of the self, or at least being less self-focused, then the truly humble person might not be attentive to his or her own actual humble qualities.

In recent years, three independent sets of researchers in separate studies concluded that most people think of humility as a personal psychological strength and that most people in the United States value this virtue. They found that people most value humility within religious seekers. It seems somehow most appropriate to seek the presence of God in humble posture. However, people do not value humility quite as much in a close partner or close friend, even though they still believe humility to be virtuous. Most of us want our close friend to be discerning enough to see faults in others (but miraculously be blind to our faults). We tend to be least accepting of humility in leaders. Most people want our leaders to have almost saintly humility, but some desire almost arrogance in our leaders.

Some people might want to appear humble—regardless of whether they act or privately feel or think of themselves as humble. Someone who wants to appear humble to others might self-consciously control prideful, arrogant, immodest, or non-humble responses—both in daily life and especially when answering a questionnaire on humility. The person might try to deceive others. The deception could be for nefarious reasons, such as to gain the confidence of an elderly investor to bilk him or her; or the deception could be innocent or naïve. The deception could even occur because the person is self-deceived about his or her humility and is acting in line with the distorted self-awareness. Thus, think of the scientist's dilemma. If all of these people are asked to rate themselves on the degree to which they are humble or arrogant, all would rate themselves inaccurately. The scientific investigator would have little way to detect the inaccuracy. Perhaps, like a navigator, the scientist could use different ways of measuring humility and triangulate on the most accurate conclusion. June Tangney concluded that the "bottom line is that the measurement of humility remains an unsolved challenge in psychology."

That was the year 2000. In the seven years since then, bright scientists have turned their minds to measuring humility. We know a few more things than we did less than a decade ago.

## MEASURING HUMILITY

Some of the most creative studies have come from the laboratory of Wade Rowatt and his collaborators at Baylor University.

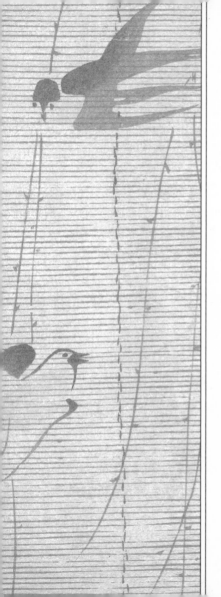

Our scientific power has outrun our spiritual power. We have guided missiles and misguided men.

—MARTIN LUTHER KING JR.

Rowatt's research group has wrestled with the difficulties in measuring humility using self-reports. In 2002, they observed that most people have a self-serving bias. This bias extends into many areas. Both married partners usually think that they give more than half to the relationship and that their spouse takes more than half. We easily see the things we contribute to the marriage but cannot see all the things done by the partner. In the workplace, we all usually feel that we are the mainstays holding the work unit together. We know what we are doing but do not accurately see the time and effort of others. On the radio program *Prairie Home Companion,* Garrison Keillor observes of his mythical town of Lake Woebegone, Minnesota, that all of the children are above average.

Not only do we believe we work harder than others, we also usually think we are smarter and more virtuous. Wade Rowatt and his colleagues used the difference between perceptions of self and others as a hidden measure of humility. They had Baylor University students estimate the degree to which they followed the Ten Commandments and two Christian commandments (love God and love others). Most students believed they followed the commandments better than other Baylor students.

Pride can clothe itself in the garments of praise or of penitence. . . . Humility . . . is the displacement of self with the enthronement of God. When God is all, self is nothing. . . . Humility is the blossom of which death to self is the perfect fruit.

—ANDREW MURRAY

The degree to which they saw themselves as better than others was taken to be a measure of low humility.

Four years later, in 2006, Wade Rowatt and several other colleagues approached the measurement of humility differently. By that time, several sound self-report measures of humility had been developed. Rowatt developed an implicit measure of humility based on how quickly people reacted to words associated with humility and arrogance. That implicit measure was related to how narcissism and high self-esteem. A straightforward rating on a "humilimeter" was related to entirely different qualities, like gratitude, forgiveness, and spiritual transcendence. Thus the way observers measure implicit attitudes and the way people describe themselves do not always tell the same story. Perhaps with humility we cannot always follow the dictum of Socrates to know ourselves.

Humble people seem to be modest and truthful. They aren't obsessed with themselves, yet have sound self-esteem. As interesting as what humility is, it is also interesting when researchers examine what humility is not.

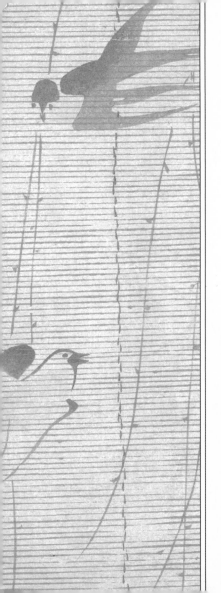

There is a principle which is a bar against all information, which is proof against all arguments and which cannot fail to keep a man in everlasting ignorance— that principle is contempt prior to investigation.

—HERBERT SPENCER

In 2004, Julie Exline, Roy Baumeister, Brad Bushman, Keith Campbell, and Eli Finkel conducted six studies showing how narcissistic entitlement, the antithesis of humility, was related to forgiveness. Entitlement was related to greater insistence on repayment (that is, revenge) after an offense and less willingness to forgive the offense. Entitlement was also negatively related to forgiving dispositions—not merely to forgiving a particular offense. In a laboratory game, "Prisoner's Dilemma," when people received a provocative message in the midst of the up-to-that-time mostly cooperative game, participants became more competitive and out for themselves. This was especially true for people with high scores in narcissistic entitlement. Those people were less willing to forgive, allocated less money to the opponent, and had less positive attitudes toward the opponent than people whose scores were lower on narcissistic entitlement. Finally, dating students who scored high in narcissistic entitlement were surveyed every two weeks for six months. They were found to be less likely to forgive their partners for transgressions. People who have a strong sense of narcissistic entitlement seem

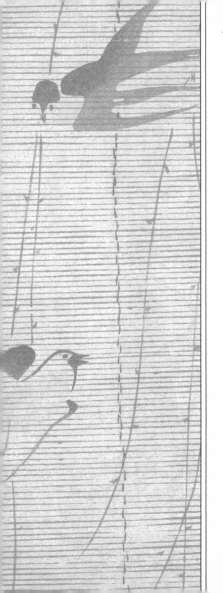

In all that surround him
the egoist sees only the
frame of his own portrait.

—J. PETIT-SENN

highly unlikely to forgive, which suggests that humble people ought to be quite willing to put the past behind them.

Finally, in 2004, researchers Keith Campbell, Angelica Bonacci, Jeremy Shelton, Julie Exline, and Brad Bushman conducted nine programmatic studies to develop a scale measuring psychological entitlement. Today, it seems that more and more people feel that they are entitled to cut us off on the interstate, cut in line at a movie, or get in the five-items-or-fewer express check-out lane when they have ten items. Campbell and his colleagues found that people who scored high on the entitlement scale believed they deserved more pay, took more selfish approaches to romantic relationships, acted in ways detrimental to friendship, were more competitive, and (get this!) were more willing to take candy that was clearly marked for children.

## SHAME, GUILT, AND THE SELF-CONSCIOUS EMOTIONS

It isn't just the self-serving bias in our nature that makes it difficult to be humble. Our upbringing introduces the gentle art of child discipline. We have to learn to be social. Correction is necessary, but taking correction is difficult for all of us. Many parents use guilt manipulation and shame induction to control their

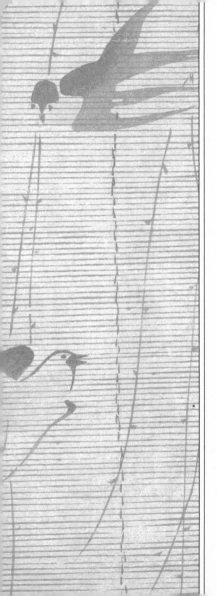

When science discovers
the center of the universe,
a lot of people will be
disappointed to find
they are not it.

**—BERNARD BAILY**

child's behavior. We often become conditioned to avoid shame and guilt in any evaluative or potentially evaluative situation. We respond to correction or criticism with feelings of shame or guilt. These self-conscious emotions are unpleasant warning signs that have become unpleasant through association with unpleasant outcomes.

Researchers who have studied self-conscious emotions, like June Tangney, have found them to be negative. The self-focused emotions also tend to direct us toward self-protection, which can undermine humility.

## HONESTY-HUMILITY AS A BASIC PART OF PERSONALITY

Michael Ashton and Kibeom Lee of Canada have identified what they call "honesty-humility" as one crucial part of personality. They found, in particular, that people high in honesty-humility were low in what is called the "dark triad of personality traits." Those traits include *psychopathy,* which is harming others without guilt, *Machiavellianism* (manipulation of others), characterized by children who lied to get their friends to eat foul-tasting cookies because they thought they could win a contest, and *narcissism.* Other research studies have shown hon-

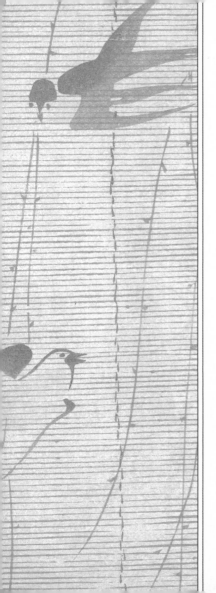

To myself, I seem to have been only like a boy playing on the seashore, diverting myself now and then finding a smoother pebble or a prettier shell than the ordinary, whilst the great ocean of truth lay all undiscovered before me.

—SIR ISAAC NEWTON

The more I enlarge the island of knowledge, the more I increase the shoreline of wonder.

—SIR ISAAC NEWTON

esty-humility to be related positively to agreeableness and to social skills like sociability and social awareness. Low scores on honesty-humility have been found to predict counterproductive school and workplace behavior. Fundamentally, this research by Ashton and Lee showed that honesty-humility was a morality-related aspect to personality.

Humility seems a part of personality. Despite the measurement difficulties noted by scientists in the year 2000, science has begun to unravel some of humility's mysteries. Nevertheless, at this point, what we know is an island of knowledge in an ocean of uncertainty.

## APPLIED PSYCHOLOGICAL SCIENCE: COUNSELING

We might think that therapists, armed with years of experience at personality assessment and helping people, can help us discern humble people. Unfortunately, that is unlikely. First, few people come to counseling to become more humble, so counselors do not get much practice helping people become more humble. Second, there are inherent mechanisms within counseling that sometimes blind the therapist to traits that are not related to psychopathology.

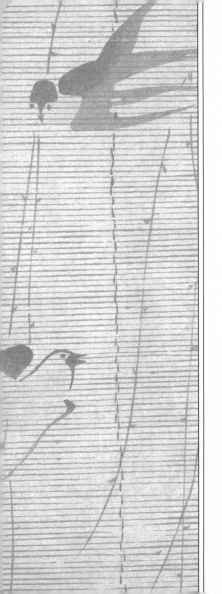

No amount of
experimentation
can ever prove me right;
a single experiment
can prove me wrong.

—ALBERT EINSTEIN

There has been much ink spilled on humility within psycho-analytic approaches to psychotherapy. Generally, these argue that humility is an essential quality of a successful psychotherapist. How can the analyst deeply understand the client if the analyst presumes to know a priori what the client's mental life is like? Like a scientist, a good counselor is wise to cultivate humility.

## LIMITATIONS OF SCIENCE

*Rena Canipe is seeing her mental faculties slip away. Some days are better than others. Some days, she phones and talks to a family member, then hangs up and phones again. Science has no answers for progressive dementia. Scientists are just beginning to unravel the causes, and have not progressed far on developing cures.*

*Even the family dynamics around dealing with progressive dementia are not well understood. Those family members who best understand are all too human. Family members have their own lives, and caring for an aging elder can require sacrifice.*

*Parents regularly sacrifice for their children who need constant care. But children progressively get more independent, stronger, more adult-like mentally and psychologically. Adult children who must care for an aging parent are faced with only the prospect that the parent is becoming*

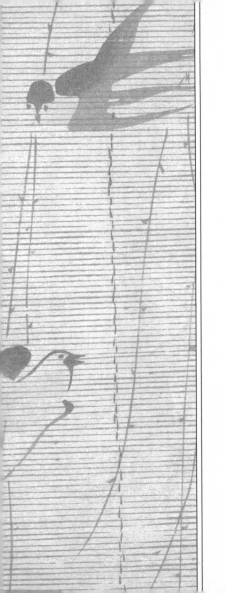

Creating without claiming,
Doing without taking
  credit,
Guiding without
  interfering,
This is primal virtue.

—TAO TE CHING

*more dependent, frailer, and less personally and mentally competent.*

*Tensions arise among family caregivers. Such tensions are inevitable. And neither social nor medical science provides answers. This can seem like a dark night of the soul for caregivers. The only answers are in sacrifice, duty, responsibility, love, compassion, and seeing the benefits of acting as a caring community to hold together the life and personhood of the elder.*

Neither counseling professionals, medical professionals, nor scientists can define universally acceptable steps to humility and happiness. Nor can they show us the skill set that makes up a humble behavioral repertoire. Is it possible for us, if we desire, to become more humble?

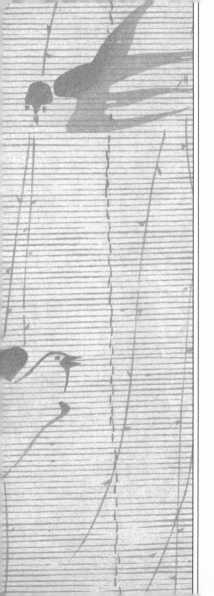

Sometimes when you sacrifice something precious, you're not really losing it. You're just passing it on to someone else.

—MITCH ALBOM

# The Spirit of Humility

RENA SPENT HER LIFE SERVING OTHERS. *Now, others are serving her. That is hard for her. But aging has a way of reversing development. Receiving help requires that we step down with the humility of a child, putting aside our adult activity of serving. This is especially difficult for a parent who must receive aid from an adult child.*

*Yet, as Rena's self slips away, to avoid the complete humiliation of loss of identity, she must accept that help. In doing so, her humility is preserved. Her personhood is held intact by her family and other helpers. They rally together. They encircle her with love. Even as Rena's personal identity and memory slide into oblivion due to progressive dementia, her humility is preserved in the collective memory of her loved ones. Her humiliation is prevented because her beloved family and helpers have drawn around her. It is they whose sacrifices give integrity to the*

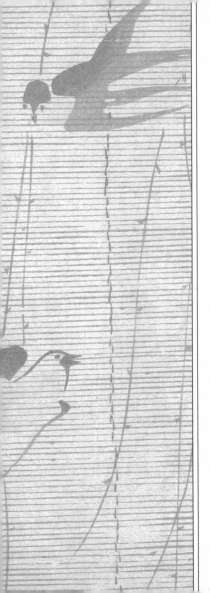

Of some thoughts one stands perplexed—especially at the sight of men's sin—and wonders whether one should use force or humble love. Always decide to use humble love. If you resolve on that, once and for all, you may subdue the whole world. Loving humility is marvelously strong, and strongest of all things, and there is nothing else like it.

—FYODOR DOSTOYEVSKY

*remaining days of Rena's life. It is their humble service that prevents Rena's humiliation.*

*The crucible formed by relationships with other people is the cradle of humility and the hedge against humiliation. In the good families— and Rena's family is a testimony to her and Clyde's parenting— humility, as shown by mutual service, is characteristic.*

In this book, we had seen that there is an inherent paradox in striving after humility. Humility can be pursued by a person, well-intentioned and having a loving heart, who wants to emulate Jesus. In the letter to the Philippians, Paul tells us, "Your attitude should be the same as Christ Jesus: . . . taking the very nature of a servant . . . he humbled himself and became obedient to death—even death on a cross!" The person who strives to be humble might try to be like Jesus by crucifying himself or herself. Yet try as he or she may, that person always has a hand free. We cannot fully reach humility by striving for it. Of all the virtues, humility might be the one that quietly shows us that, in a fundamental way, there is no dividing line between the arrogant and the humble, between the proud and the modest; none can achieve humility alone.

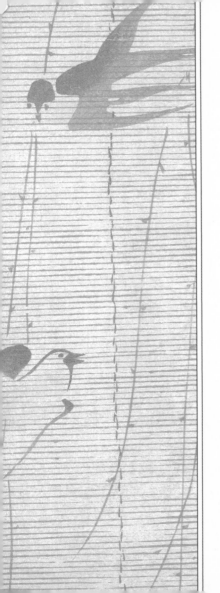

Go sweep out the chamber
of your heart.
Make it ready to be the
dwelling place of
the beloved.
When you depart out,
He will enter it.
In you, void of yourself, will
He display His beauties.

—MAHMUD SHABISTARI

Good and evil indeed pass through each of our hearts. Our efforts to be humble are undermined all too often by that villain, our own heart.

Being humble, then, is like trying to catch air in our hands. The faster we close our fingers around it, the faster the air spurts away. The slower that we close our hands, the slower the air spurts away. But if we hold our hands, palms up, arms outstretched, then air will come to rest in our hands. To experience humility, then, is not to grasp or to strive toward it, but to rest as we seek to bless others. When we are moved from within, a humble spirit can descend upon us like that air resting in the open hand.

Aspiring to humility is forcing the hand closed and clenching the fist. Aspiring to achieve humility is King Kong with his fists clenched, beating his chest, bellowing and calling attention to himself.

However, humility is a spiritual activity. It is opening the hands in love, extending the hands outward to other people, extending the open hands upwards to God, and receiving in an open heart the spirit of humility. Humility is letting that spirit come into us and energize our hands to be helping hands.

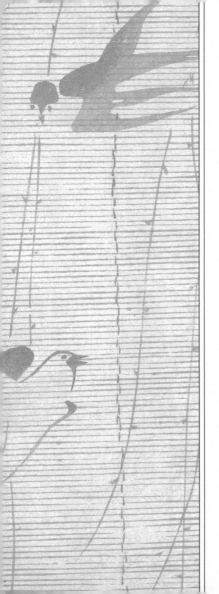

We must speak with
all the humility that is
appropriate to our limited
vision, but we must speak.

—MARTIN LUTHER KING JR.


There is no limit to what
can be done if it doesn't
matter who gets the credit.

—AUTHOR UNKNOWN

Humility is inspiring. It inspires us as we intake the spirit of humility. And humility within us can inspire others.

This is the spirit of humility that we seek. It is not something we achieve but something we receive. If we try to meet the needs of other people, then someday perhaps someone may secretly nominate us as a hero in his or her Hall of Humility. May we each receive this simple spirit of humility. May we grow in trust that our own needs are met so that we may seek to understand and try to meet the needs of others. Perhaps, a few may secretly nominate us as a hero in their Hall of Humility. We will not know. We will know only those faces in our own Hall of Humility, and we will draw great strength from their hidden lives.

Humility is a Pegasus that serves others. It is bridled with grace and modesty. It rises to the heavens bearing others to a higher life. It is others who recognize and appreciate the love, power, and accomplishments of the Pegasus, humility, not the winged horse itself. For humility is the quiet virtue.

# References

Ashton, M. C., Lee, K., de Vries, R. E., Perugini, M., Gnisci, A., & Sergi, I. (2006) The HEXACO model of personality structure and indigenous lexical personality dimensions in Italian, Dutch, and English. *Journal of Personality Assessment, 40,* 851–75.

Campbell, W. K., Bonacci, A. M., Shelton, J., Exline, J. J., & Bushman, B. J. (2004). Psychological entitlement: Interpersonal consequences and validation of a self-report measure. *Journal of Personality Assessment, 83,* 29–45.

Costa, P. T., Jr., McRae, R. R., & Jonsson, F. H. (2002). Validity and utility of the revised NEO personality inventory: Examples from Europe. In B. de Raad & M. Perugini (Eds.), *Big five assessment.* Cambridge, MA: Hogrefe & Huber.

Exline, J. J., Baumeister, R. F., Bushman, B. J., Campbell, W. K., & Finkel, E. J. (2004). Too proud to let go: Narcissistic entitlement as a barrier to forgiveness. *Journal of Personality and Social Psychology, 87,* 894–912.

Exline, J. J., & Geyer, A. L. (2004). Perceptions of humility: a preliminary study. *Self and Identity, 3,* 95–114.

Greenwald, A. G., McGhee, D. E., & Schwartz, J. L. K. (1998). Measuring individual differences in implicit cognition: The Implicit Associations Test. *Journal of Personality and Social Psychology, 74,* 1464–80.

Hareli, S., & Weiner, B. (2000). Accounts for success as determinants of perceived arrogance and modesty. *Motivation and Emotion, 24,* 215–36.

Rowatt, W. C., Ottenbriet, A., Nesselroade, K. P., Jr., & Cunningham, P. A. (2002). On being holier-than-though or humbler-than-thee: A social-psychological perspective on religiousness and humility. *Journal for the Scientific Study of Religion, 41,* 227–37.

Rowatt, W. C., Powers, C., Targhetta, V., Comer, J., Kennedy, S., & Labouff, J. (2006). Development and initial validation of an implicit measure of humility relative to arrogance. *Journal of Positive Psychology, 1,* 198–211.

Tangney, J. P. (2000). Humility: Theoretical perspectives, empirical findings and directions for future research. *Journal of Social & Clinical Psychology, 19,* 70–82. The quote from chapter five, "What Does Science Tell Us about Humility?," is found on page 419.

# Select Books about Humility

Bonomo, C. (2003). *Humble pie: St. Benedict's ladder of humility.* Harrisburg, PA: Morehouse Publishing.

Cooper, D. (2002). *The measure of things: Humanism, humility, and mystery.* Oxford: Oxford University Press.

Delio, I. (2005). *The humility of God: A Franciscan perspective.* Cincinnati, OH: St. Anthony Messenger Press.

Elmer, D. (2006). *Cross-cultural servanthood: Serving the world in Christlike humility.* Downers Grove, IL: InterVarsity Press.

Jones, T., & Fontenot, M. (2003). *The prideful soul's guide to humility.* Billerica, MA: Discipleship Publications International.

Mahaney, C. J., & Harris, J. (2005). *Humility: True greatness.* Sisters, OR: Multnomah.

Murray, A. (2002). *Humility: The journey toward holiness.* New Kensington, PA: Whitaker House.

# About the Author

DR. EVERETT WORTHINGTON has dedicated his life to the study and teaching of forgiveness and justice and how they come together, as well as marriage and family-related topics. As a professor of psychology at Virginia Commonwealth University (VCU), he has taught at VCU's American Psychological Association-accredited psychology program for almost thirty years. A prolific writer and producer of multimedia resources, Dr. Worthington has published twenty-two books on forgiveness, religion, and marriage and family topics. He has also published over two hundred scientific articles and scholarly chapters and produced numerous multimedia resources. An international speaker, Dr. Worthington has won recognition for his research and teaching. No stranger to the media, Dr.

Worthington and his work have been featured on numerous television and radio programs and in newspapers and magazines. He founded a professional journal and served as its editor for seven years, and he served as executive director of the John Templeton Foundation's "A Campaign for Forgiveness Research" from its inception until December 2005. Dr. Worthington describes his mission as "to bring forgiveness into every willing heart, home, or homeland."